# Loving v. Virginia

## Interracial Marriage

### Karen Alonso

Landmark Supreme Court Cases

**Enslow Publishers, Inc.**

| 40 Industrial Road | PO Box 38 |
|---|---|
| Box 398 | Aldershot |
| Berkeley Heights, NJ 07922 | Hants GU12 6BP |
| USA | UK |

http://www.enslow.com

Library of Congress Cataloging-in-Publication Data

Alonso, Karen.
  Loving v. Virginia : interracial marriage / Karen Alonso.
      p. cm. – (Landmark Supreme Court cases)
  Includes bibliographical references and index.
  Summary: Explores the Supreme Court case that challenged and eventually
  overturned Virginia's law forbidding interracial marriages.
      ISBN 0-7660-1338-3
      1. Loving, Richard Perry—Trials, litigation, etc.—Juvenile
  literature. 2. Loving, Mildred Jeter—Trials, litigation,
  etc—Juvenile literature. 3. Miscegenation—Law and
  legislation—Virginia—Juvenile literature. [1. Loving, Richard
  Perry—Trials, litigation, etc. 2. Loving, Mildred Jeter—Trials,
  litigation, etc. 3. Interracial marriage.] I. Title: Loving versus
  Virginia. II. Title. III. Series.
      KF224.L68 A44   2000
      346.7301'6—dc21
                                                      99-050541

Printed in the United States of America

10 9 8 7 6 5 4 3 2 1

To Our Readers:
All Internet addresses in this book were active and appropriate when we went to press. Any comments or suggestions can be sent by e-mail to Comments@enslow.com or to the address on the back cover.

Photo Credits: CORBIS/Bettmann, pp. 7, 20, 36, 41, 43, 57 (bottom right), 59, 80, 95; CORBIS/Flip Schulke, pp. 40, 57 (top left, top right), 62; CORBIS/ G. E. Kidder Smith, p. 49; CORBIS/Hulton-Deutsch Collection, p. 29; CORBIS/ Ted Streshinsky, p. 57 (bottom left); Reproduced from the collections of the Library of Congress, p. 19; National Archives, p. 22.

Cover Photo: CORBIS/Roman Soumar

# Contents

# Author's Note

For many reasons, this was a difficult book to write. One reason was that this case often shows the worst side of human nature. It also reminds us of many stressful periods in our nation's history, as society struggled (and sometimes still struggles) with the issue of racial equality.

Another painful realization is that an enormous amount of effort has been made by some lawmakers and social leaders to keep a very definite line of division between the races. We may think of our state lawmakers as leaders who are meant to erase those lines by passing laws that encourage equality. When they fail in this duty, we are all the more disappointed.

Still, not *all* lawmakers, citizens, and judges are to blame for the laws and attitudes described in this book. Others have done just as much to open communication and create harmony. That is what is best about Richard and Mildred Loving's story—that history is made up of individuals—and the choices they make. That is the way the Lovings looked at the world and at their neighbors. In the same way, we can all be a part of our country's history through the choices we make. I challenge you to follow the example of Richard and Mildred Loving, by welcoming each new person you meet as an individual.

# Introduction

On the night of July 13, 1958, Richard and Mildred Loving were asleep in their home in Central Point, a tiny village in rural Virginia.[1] The Lovings were newlyweds, having been married in Washington, D.C., just five weeks earlier. However, the peace of the country night was broken when Sheriff Garnett Brooks and two deputies arrived at the Lovings' home at 2:00 A.M.

The three officers of the law threw open the unlocked door, and made their way to Richard and Mildred's bedroom. The noise made by the men and the light from three flashlights woke the Lovings from their sound sleep. Mr. and Mrs. Loving were placed under arrest. How could the Lovings know that when they left their home with the sheriff that night they would be entering the fight for equal rights that was sweeping the country?

Richard Perry Loving and Mildred Jeter Loving were arrested for committing a felony, a serious kind of crime. Husband and wife were brought to the county jail, where they stayed for five days. The family arranged for Richard and Mildred to be released on bail. By posting bail, or depositing a sum of money with the court, the Lovings could return home while they waited for their trial. Under this arrangement, they would not have to return to jail unless they were found guilty. No one knew, however, that the Lovings' troubles had just begun.

What was the serious crime the Lovings had committed? If you could have been there that night and looked into the jail cells at the Lovings, it would have been difficult to see what harm this couple could have presented to society. Richard was a brick mason who enjoyed racing cars on country roads near his home.[2] Mildred was a slender woman with a lovely smile.[3] She was so tall that she had earned the nickname "Stringbean" during her childhood. Some just called her "Bean," for short.

Richard and Mildred both grew up in Central Point, Virginia, where their families had lived for generations. Both considered themselves "country people" who enjoyed being close to their families. Their home was in rural Virginia, between Richmond and Fredericksburg.

However, the Lovings' crime had less to do with what the couple had done than with who they were. Richard Loving was a white man. Mildred Loving was part African American and part American Indian. In 1958 in Virginia there was a state law that made it a crime for a white person to marry a person of color.

Similar laws were in force in fifteen other states:

Mildred and Richard Loving are shown here following their marriage. Their love endured despite a law that tried to keep them apart. Following their arrest in their own bedroom for the crime of being married, they struggled for nine years to have their marriage legally recognized in Virginia.

Alabama, Arkansas, Delaware, Florida, Georgia, Kentucky, Louisiana, Mississippi, Missouri, North Carolina, Oklahoma, South Carolina, Tennessee, Texas, and West Virginia.

Virginia was so serious about enforcing its laws that an interracial couple could be sentenced to one to five years in prison. Virginia's law against interracial marriages had been on the books, in one form or another, since colonial times. Mildred and Richard Loving's trial would give Virginia courts an opportunity to say that the time had come to do away with this unjust state law.

Would the court in Caroline County, Virginia, seize that opportunity? The answer would make a great deal of difference to the newlywed couple. Either they would be allowed to enjoy married life in peace among family and friends, or they would have to serve additional time in jail. The final answer would not come for nearly ten years.

# 1

# Laws Against Interracial Marriage

The history of this country's attitude toward interracial marriages began almost as soon as the first slaves arrived in Colonial America. As early as 1691, the Colony of Virginia passed a law against what would later become known as miscegenation (miss-uh-jen-ay-shun), or mixed marriages. This term comes from the combination of two Latin words *miscere*, or mix, and *genus*, meaning race.

The term was coined by American David Goodman Croly in 1864. Croly had written a pamphlet titled "Miscegenation: The Theory of the Blending of the Races" (although, interestingly, he did not sign his name to it). In the pamphlet, Croly wrote in favor of mixed marriages, even though he personally did not believe that the races should intermarry. The pamphlet was meant as a political trick. Croly, a Democrat, hoped to affect the 1864 presidential election race between Abraham Lincoln and George McClellan. Croly tried to make race an issue in the election by making it appear that the Republican party had published the pamphlet in support of miscegenation. He expected readers to be outraged by the claims made in the pamphlet, which in turn would encourage readers to support the Democrats.[1] Croly's pamphlet included statements that supported the idea that history showed mixed races to be "superior, mentally, physically, and morally, to those pure or unmixed."[2] Croly also wrote that wherever unmixed peoples lived, he found evidence of "decay both in the mental and physical powers."[3] Although Croly did not actually mean to support miscegenation, those who favored mixed marriages used Croly's arguments to support their position.

Croly's pamphlet obviously would not have received a warm welcome in Colonial Virginia. The taboo against the mixing of races was too firmly in place. Antimiscegenation laws clearly outlawed marriages between people of different races. In Colonial Virginia, white people were not allowed to marry anyone other than another white person. People of African descent were permitted to marry other people of African descent, American Indians, and mulattos—people who had one black parent and one white parent.

Colonists opposed mixed marriages for a number of reasons. One reason may simply have been economic. The children of these marriages might have expected to be free, or might begin to think of themselves as free people. This would challenge the social order established by the slaveholders, which determined that such people and their children were meant to be slaves.[4] Traditional English law was generally observed in Colonial Virginia. Under that law, a child was born either slave or free, according to the *father's* status. This would mean, however, that thousands of children born to slave women could have been born free—if their fathers were white. This would have meant a very large loss of "property" for the slavemaster. Colonists avoided this loss by changing the law. Now all children born to a black woman were either slave or free, based upon the *mother's* status. Thus, the slaveholder's "property" increased with each birth. Sadly, this meant that thousands of babies were born into slavery.[5]

## A Matter of Racism

Another reason that many Virginia colonists opposed miscegenation was simple racism. Many white Virginians held "blacks, as a people and as a class, in contempt."[6]

Considered to be something less than human by white colonists, blacks mattered little. "Decisions were to be made for them, not by them."[7] Other colonists even continued to see blacks as "subhuman." Their creation meant that they were doomed to be slaves.[8]

Since the black slaves were not considered to be human, or at least less human than whites, intermarriage was unthinkable. From the outset, Virginia lawmakers had made the purpose of their law against miscegenation very clear. Virginians considered the idea of children born from such marriages to be offensive. The law was originally meant to prevent "that abominable mixture and spurious issue which may hereafter increase by negroes, mulattoes, and Indians intermarrying with English, or other white women."[9] (Of course, the idea of a marriage between a black woman and a white man was equally outrageous.)

Clearly, Virginians considered the idea of children born of such marriages to be offensive. In order to deter mixed marriages and thus an increased number of mixed-race children, the state established stiff penalties for the parties involved in interracial marriages.

## Penalties for Intermarriage

Under Virginia's law, any marriage between a white person and a black person or an American Indian, was not a marriage at all. It did not matter whether an interracial couple held a traditional or religious ceremony. The colonial government did not have to process a divorce for these couples, since the law made these unions "void."

Although such marriages were legally void, Virginia also made it a crime for a minister to go through the process of performing a marriage ceremony for an interracial couple. The fine for the minister who did so was set at ten thousand pounds of tobacco. (Tobacco was used for money in Colonial Virginia.) Half of the fine was paid to the King of England, and the other half was paid to the person who informed the authorities about the minister's actions.

Harsh penalties were ordered for a mixed couple who lived together as husband and wife. The black partner in a mixed marriage was probably too valuable as a piece of property to be hurt or driven from the community. However, under early colonial laws, the white partner of an interracial marriage was banished from the Colony.[10] This penalty lets us see how much interracial marriages disgusted American colonists. With living conditions so difficult in Colonial America, separation from the community made survival almost impossible. Any children born of such marriages were labeled *colored* or *mulatto* and were taken from their mother. They were sold into indentured servitude until they reached the age of thirty.[11] Indentured servants had a contract to work without pay for a master for four to seven years. Once the contracted time was up, they were free. They were considered to be on the same social level as slaves.

Because all people born of parents of different races were looked down upon by whites as inferior beings, blacks and mulattos were treated with little respect.[12] With such an attitude, the stage was set for the making of American laws to treat black Americans differently from white Americans.

## Virginia Develops Antimiscegenation Laws

Long after the American colonies won their independence from England, Virginia kept its laws forbidding mixed marriages. Systems were developed to make sure that no mixed marriages were performed. For instance, in 1853, just before the Civil War, Virginia lawmakers demanded that a "certificate" file be kept of the ancestry of all Virginia citizens.[13] The certificate would show whether an individual had African-American or Indian blood.

By 1866, Virginia had laws that said that anyone who had "one-fourth or more of negro blood, shall be deemed a colored person," and that those who were not "colored" but had "one-fourth or more of Indian blood, shall be deemed an Indian."[14]

This law remained unchanged until 1910 when a colored person was described as someone with one-sixteenth or more African-American blood. As before, it was illegal for a black person to marry a white person. This meant that if you lived in Virginia in 1910 and had a great-great-grandparent who was fully of African descent, you would be considered "colored" and could not marry the person of your choice, if that person were "white."[15]

In 1924, Virginia changed its law again. This version changed the focus of the law against mixed marriages. Although Virginia continued to identify a "colored person" as anyone with one-sixteenth or more of "non-white" blood, there was an additional restriction. Now white people were not allowed to marry anyone with "any trace whatsoever of any blood other than Caucasian."[16]

The 1924 change to the law also made it a crime for a mixed couple to leave the state of Virginia for the purpose of marrying, and then returning to Virginia to live there as a married couple. This portion of the law was called the "evasion statute," because couples had evaded, or avoided, Virginia's law by leaving the state.

The 1924 law against miscegenation was the version that was in effect when Richard and Mildred Loving became husband and wife. The exact language of Section 20–58 of Virginia's law was indeed grim and threatening:

> If any white person and colored person shall go out of this State, for the purpose of being married, and with the intention of returning, and be married out of it, and afterwards return to and reside in it, [living together] as man and wife, they shall be punished as provided in Section 20–59.[17]

Section 20–59 of Virginia's law prescribed the penalty for intermarriage:

> If any white person intermarry with a colored person, or any colored person intermarry with a white person, he shall be guilty of a felony and shall be punished by confinement in the penitentiary for not less than one nor more than five years.[18]

The 1924 law affected a greater number of people than the earlier versions of the antimiscegenation law. Under the 1910 version, a white person and a "colored person" with less than one-sixteenth "negro" blood, could marry. The new version said that a white person could only marry a person who could prove that he or she was *fully* "white."

Oddly enough, Virginia's laws against race mixing did not apply to members of nonwhite races. Therefore, a person of American Indian ancestry was free to marry a person of Chinese ancestry, or a person of any other nonwhite ancestry.

In the sixteen states with laws banning mixed marriages, lawmakers had imagined the white race to be "pure." Trying to maintain that purity led to intricate laws. Their arbitrary definitions of white or "colored" led to bizarre results. For instance, as a result of different state laws, a person could be considered legally white in Florida but black in Georgia. Mixed-race people in Arizona were not permitted to marry anyone—even another person of mixed race.[19]

As we have seen, the laws against mixed marriages became more restrictive. Instead of treating all of its citizens as equals, Virginia's laws seemed to be aimed at dividing the races whenever possible.

Virginia lawmakers, and those of fifteen other American states, failed to recognize even as late as the 1960s, the value of all people as individuals, regardless of race.

## Jim Crow Enters American History

Even before Virginia developed the 1924 version of the law that affected Mildred and Richard Loving, another category of laws emerged, its specific purpose to treat blacks as inferior to whites. When the Civil War ended in 1865, many white Americans resisted the fact that black Americans were free. This was even true despite the fact that the Fourteenth Amendment, enacted in 1868, declared African Americans to be equal citizens of the United States. This new amendment also prohibited any state from taking away any of the privileges of being an American citizen. No state was to take away life, liberty, or property without some kind of legal proceeding. The amendment also required that all citizens be treated equally by the legal system. This concept is known as equal protection under the law.

Enacted in 1870, the Fifteenth Amendment prohibited the United States, or any of the individual states, from preventing any citizen from voting because of race, color, or the fact that they had at one time been a slave. Unfortunately, these amendments failed to provide the freed slaves with the full enjoyment of their status as citizens.

Following the Civil War, many of the Southern and border states replaced the chains of slavery with new laws that were designed to keep black Americans in a lower social level than white Americans. These laws came to be known as "Black Codes," or "Jim Crow Laws." Jim Crow Laws affected almost every aspect of life in the South. Blacks were not allowed to send their children to school with white children, or to sit in the

The Thirteenth Amendment to the United States Constitution outlawed slavery. This 1866 engraving shows African Americans celebrating the passage of the Thirteenth Amendment.

front seats of a bus. Public drinking fountains were marked "For Whites Only," or "For Colored Only."

Under the Black Codes, African Americans in 1873 were forbidden to

> appear in the towns [other than as] menial servants. They were required to reside on and [farm] the soil without the right to purchase or own it. They were excluded from many [professions], and were not permitted to give testimony in the courts of any case where a white man was a party. It was said that their

Jim Crow Laws or Black Codes kept the races apart. Separate facilities were kept for whites and blacks in public places. Here, an elderly man is leaving the waiting room for African Americans in a bus station in Jackson, Mississippi, sometime in the 1950s.

lives were at the mercy of bad men, either because the laws for their protection were insufficient or were not enforced.[20]

Some of the "bad men" who enforced the Black Codes were members of the Ku Klux Klan (KKK).[21] The first Ku Klux Klan, formed shortly after the Civil War, opposed the advancement of African Americans. A second Klan—formed in 1915—expanded its focus of hatred to include Jews and other minority groups. And it used terror, beatings, and even murder when it felt that these minority groups were not keeping to their "place" in society.

Even in recent times, "Klansmen" covered themselves with hoods and white robes when they assembled to voice opposition to some supposed intrusion on the rights of the white race. A black family moving into a "white" neighborhood, or the hiring of a black worker rather than a white one could spark a demonstration by the KKK. The demonstrations have ranged from a parade of Klansmen in their hooded uniforms, to placing a burning cross on the front lawn of the offender, to more violent demonstrations.

The United States Congress attempted to end this form of oppressing the freed slaves by passing the Ku Klux Klan Act in 1871. As a federal law, the Klan Act applied to the entire country, not specific individual

What some state lawmakers could not accomplish with Jim Crow Laws, the Ku Klux Klan tried to accomplish through intimidation and violence.

states. Any state law that contradicts a federal law can be declared unconstitutional by a federal court. This particular federal law made it a crime for a group to gather and to plan to deprive a class of people of equal protection of the laws, as was promised by the Fourteenth Amendment to the Constitution.

Sadly, all these new laws did little to change the treatment of African Americans in the South. Despite federal laws that forbid such behavior, some white Americans continued to keep themselves separate from black Americans. Segregation and discrimination remained the rule, particularly in the southern states. Jim Crow Laws had become so much a part of American life that they survived nearly one hundred years after the Civil War.

By the time Mildred and Richard Loving were confronted with Virginia's antimiscegenation law, they also faced almost a century of a nation's stubborn refusal to accept African Americans as fellow Americans.

# 2

# The Road to the Supreme Court

The Lovings met at a local dance in Caroline County, Virginia, and enjoyed a long courtship. Unfortunately, the difficulties for Mildred and Richard began at the time they decided to marry. It was illegal for anyone authorized by the state of Virginia to perform marriage ceremonies to do so for an interracial couple.

Mildred and Richard Loving had known that they could not marry legally in Virginia, so they decided to travel to Washington, D.C., for their wedding ceremony on June 2, 1958. Richard was twenty-four years old and Mildred was eighteen. What they were not aware of was that they would not be allowed to return to Virginia to live there in peace as husband and wife.

The newlywed couple returned to Virginia within a month. However, it was not long before a grand jury decided that the Lovings should be charged with violating Virginia's ban on interracial marriage. Although a grand jury does not decide a defendant's guilt or innocence, it does decide whether a person should be charged with a crime and required to stand trial. On July 11, 1958, a warrant was issued for the arrest of Richard Loving and Mildred Jeter for the crime of living together as husband and wife "against the peace and dignity of the Commonwealth of Virginia."[1] Sheriff Garnett Brooks arrested Richard and Mildred on July 13, 1958. The couple had to remain in jail until friends and family could arrange for bail. Five days later, the Lovings were released on $1,000 bond until their trial.[2] Bond is an amount of money deposited with the court to ensure that the defendant returns for a trial or other hearing.

Richard and Mildred Loving waited six months for their trial. On January 6, 1959, they appeared in court and were arraigned, or informed of the specific charges against them. The Lovings were asked if they claimed to be "guilty" or "not guilty" of breaking Virginia's antimiscegenation law. Before Judge Leon M. Bazile, Richard and Mildred pleaded "not guilty."

At the same time, the couple waived, or voluntarily

gave up their right, to a trial before a jury. This meant that Judge Bazile would have the sole responsibility of hearing the evidence, and of deciding whether the Lovings had committed a crime under Virginia law.

## Banished

After all evidence was presented, Richard and Mildred decided to change their plea from "not guilty" to "guilty," in order to escape a jail sentence.[3] Judge Bazile accepted the change of plea and set the sentence, or punishment, for both Richard and Mildred Loving at one year in jail. At the same time, the judge suspended the Lovings' sentence for a period of twenty-five years. Under this arrangement, the judge would not actually send the Lovings to prison for their one-year sentence if one condition was met. That condition was that Mildred and Richard had to leave Virginia immediately.

The couple was banished from their home state and not allowed to "return together or at the same time . . . for a period of 25 years."[4] The situation must have seemed hopeless to Richard and Mildred. As Judge Bazile looked down from the bench at the young couple, he used the opportunity to voice his opinion on mixed marriages.

> Almighty God created the races white, black, yellow . . .
> and red, and he placed them on separate continents.

26

And but for the interference with His arrangement there would be no cause for such marriages. The fact that he separated the races shows that he did not intend for the races to mix.[5]

Judge Bazile then attempted to make Richard and Mildred Loving aware of the "awfulness" of their offense.[6] The judge reminded the defendants that such "unnatural alliances" were a felony, or the most serious level of crime possible, under Virginia's law. "Conviction of a felony is a serious matter. You lose your political rights; and only the government has the power to restore them . . . And as long as you live you will be known as a felon."[7]

Such words from a judge must have led the defendants to think that there was little hope of their ever living together as husband and wife in Virginia. The Lovings faced a terrible choice: leave the comfort of their families and familiar surroundings, simply so that they could live together in peace as a married couple, or live separately. When Mildred and Richard were released from custody, they left the courthouse with no idea what the future held for them, or their new marriage.

## The Appeal Process

Mildred and Richard Loving returned to Washington, D.C., and set up their household. The coming years would bring three children: Sidney, Donald, and Peggy, but Mildred and Richard still missed their families. Mildred, in particular, wanted to raise the children in open spaces. She "missed . . . walking on grass instead of concrete."[8]

Finally, the Loving family decided that they could not adjust to city life. With the threat of a prison sentence still hanging over their heads, Richard and Mildred decided to risk returning to Virginia. For years, the Lovings stayed in Caroline County and lived a secret life. Friends and family protected them from arrest, but Richard would later say "it was right rough."[9] Finally, in 1963, Mildred Loving sent a letter to the United States attorney general, Robert Kennedy, asking for help.

As attorney general, Robert Kennedy was the head of the United States Department of Justice and represented the United States in legal matters. He also gave advice to the president and to the heads of different departments of the government. Robert Kennedy could not represent the Lovings in court, but he did send Mildred Loving's letter to the Virginia branch of the American Civil Liberties Union (ACLU).

The ACLU was formed in 1920 in order to protect the rights guaranteed to American citizens under the Bill of Rights, the first ten amendments to the United States Constitution. These civil rights include the right to a fair trial, the right to free speech, and the right of all citizens to be treated equally under the law. What the ACLU seeks to do is enforce constitutional rights. Additionally, it does not ask for payment from those clients who cannot afford legal services.[10]

The ACLU sent two Virginia lawyers, Bernard S. Cohen and Philip J. Hirschkop, to assist the Lovings in their case against the state of Virginia. On November 6, 1963, Cohen and Hirschkop filed a motion in Virginia state trial court on behalf of the Lovings. The motion asked the state trial court to vacate, or reverse the judgment, and set aside the sentence that Judge Bazile had imposed on the Lovings. The lawyers made this motion

Attorney General Robert Kennedy, brother of President John F. Kennedy is shown here. Mildred Loving wrote to Robert Kennedy, asking for help. Kennedy referred her letter to the American Civil Liberties Union (ACLU).

on the grounds that the Virginia laws were "repugnant to the Fourteenth Amendment."[11]

Section 1 of the Fourteenth Amendment provides that

> [a]ll persons born . . . in the United States . . . are citizens of the United States and of the State wherein they reside. No State shall make or enforce any law which shall abridge the privileges or immunities of citizens of the United States; nor shall any State deprive any person of life, liberty, or property, without due process of law; nor deny to any person within its jurisdiction the equal protection of the laws.

On January 22, 1965, the state trial judge denied the motion to vacate the sentences.[12] This was to be expected. In the motion to vacate their sentence, Richard and Mildred Loving essentially were asking Judge Bazile, or one of his fellow judges, to change the sentence that he had already imposed. Judge Bazile had already made his disapproval of mixed marriages quite clear.

The Lovings' next appealed to the Supreme Court of Appeals of Virginia. That court upheld the constitutionality of the antimiscegenation laws. However, the Supreme Court of Appeals of Virginia did invalidate the sentence that Judge Bazile had imposed on the Lovings. The court declared Bazile's sentence to an "exile" for twenty-five years to be "so unreasonable as to render the sentences void."[13]

The Supreme Court of Appeals of Virginia, Virginia's highest court, then remanded, or sent back the case to the trial court on March 7, 1966, so that the trial court could impose a different, less extreme, sentence on the Lovings.[14]

Later that same month, on March 28, Virginia's Supreme Court of Appeals entered another order that suspended any action on the Lovings' case in Virginia courts. This order gave the Lovings time to appeal to the United States Supreme Court.[15] The Lovings were now able to ask the United States Supreme Court to decide whether Virginia's law against miscegenation was unconstitutional. While the Lovings' attorneys were making an appeal to the United States Supreme Court, the trial court in Virginia could not change its sentence or impose a new sentence on the couple.

On December 12, 1966, the Supreme Court of the United States informed Richard and Mildred Loving that it would consider the constitutionality of Virginia's antimiscegenation law. Because of the serious nature of the Lovings' claim that they had been denied due process, and equal protection of the laws, the United States Supreme Court agreed to hear the appeal. However, the simple fact that the Supreme Court had agreed to hear the Lovings' appeal did not mean that the case had been won. The Lovings and their attorneys still had to convince the Supreme Court that Virginia's law was unconstitutional.

Attorneys Cohen and Hirschkop looked at the long history of race-related Supreme Court decisions. They must have known that their presentation of the Lovings' case would be a struggle. They would have to face not only centuries of prejudice against mixed marriages, but also the long history of Supreme Court decisions that supported antimiscegenation laws.

Chief Justice Earl Warren and the rest of the Court were making great strides toward supporting the civil rights movement, but a number of earlier Supreme Court cases that did not support the Lovings' position were still in effect, or "good law." Cohen and Hirschkop faced the enormous task of convincing the Supreme Court to abolish one of the remaining laws that separated black Americans from the same treatment under the law that white Americans enjoyed.

# 3

# A Look at Race-Related Laws

Over the years, the Supreme Court has handed down a
number of opinions on state laws that allowed different
treatment for different races. This was especially true
when the law in question involved relationships
between two people of different races. The opinions of
the Supreme Court in these particular cases would provide precedent, or guidance, to the current Supreme
Court when it considered the Lovings' case.

There were three important cases that the Supreme
Court might turn to for guidance. These cases were
*Pace* v. *Alabama*[1], *McLaughlin* v. *Florida*[2], and *Naim* v.
*Naim*.[3] *Pace* v. *Alabama* was a case that went all the way
back to 1882.

In that case, the state of Alabama had a law that made it illegal for unmarried partners to engage in sexual relations. However, the penalty was greater if the "guilty parties" included one white person and one black person. The penalty was less severe if the "crime" was committed by two people of the same race.

The United States Supreme Court upheld Alabama's law. The Court reasoned that the law could not be said to discriminate against people of color, because the punishment for each participant was the same, regardless of his or her race. According to the court then, this was equal application of the law.[4]

## Virginia's Courts Address Mixed Marriages

In 1955, the Virginia Supreme Court reviewed the constitutionality of laws that applied to mixed race couples. *Naim* v. *Naim* was the first major challenge to the constitutionality of Virginia's law against mixed marriages. *Naim* was not a criminal case. It involved a suit to annul a marriage between a white woman and her Chinese husband. Annulment ends a marriage. Unlike divorce, however, which also ends a marriage, an annulment decrees that the marriage never existed.

In this case, Ham Say Naim and Ruby Elaine Naim left Virginia to be married in North Carolina, which had no law against interracial marriages. Mr. and Mrs.

Naim then returned to Virginia to live there as husband and wife. Fifteen months later, Ruby Naim filed for annulment, but her husband wanted to keep the marriage together.[5] The Virginia state court granted the annulment to Mrs. Naim, stating that the state had a "legitimate purpose" in ending mixed marriages. That purpose was "to preserve the racial integrity of its citizens," and to prevent "the corruption of blood," "a mongrel breed of citizens," and "the obliteration of racial pride."[6]

This was a very clear statement from Virginia's court that, in its view, nonwhite Americans were inferior to white Americans, and that the white race should not be diminished by mixing with any other race. However, a less than obvious statement would come from the United States Supreme Court when Mr. Naim appealed the state court's decision to the highest court in the nation.

Only months before Mr. Naim's appeal reached the United States Supreme Court, that court had decided *Brown* v. *Board of Education*, which made segregation, or separation of the races, in public schools illegal.[7] The Supreme Court Justices who decided *Brown* were led by Chief Justice Earl Warren. Chief Justice Warren was the strongest supporter of racial equality. Throughout his time on the bench, Warren did more than any other judge in American history to make sure that the law was applied equally.[8] *Brown* was a bold move on the Supreme Court's part, signaling the end to the last traces of the slave laws. The *Brown* decision may have led Mr. Naim's attorneys to think that the Supreme Court was ready to strike down miscegenation laws, but they were mistaken.

Only four of the Supreme Court Justices were willing to hear the *Naim* appeal. Unfortunately for Mr. Naim, a majority of Justices must consider the case important enough to be reviewed by all of the Justices on the Supreme Court. Justices Warren, Black, Douglas, and Reed voted to review the lower court's decision,

Chief Justice Earl Warren did more than any other judge in American history to make sure that the Constitution was applied equally to all citizens.

and consider the constitutionality of antimiscegenation laws. However, Justices Clark and Frankfurter were more concerned with what they had already accomplished. If the laws against intermarriage were struck down so soon after making segregation illegal, some of the Justices feared that many Americans might show greater resistance to integration, or the mixing of the races.

This fear was not without justification. The idea of intermarriage still remained as a matter of deep concern for many Americans. Many felt that integration in schools would only encourage the "problem" of interracial marriage. One white man from Alabama expressed his fear,

> How do we know, if we shove our kids in schools together, our white girls won't get so used to being around nigras [Negroes] that after a while they won't pay no attention to color? Then pretty soon they will be socializing together, dancing all hugged up, and the next thing they'll be at the altar.[9]

Since the *Naim* appeal lacked the necessary support of a majority of Justices in order to be granted review before the Supreme Court, the decision of Virginia's Court of Appeals remained the final decision on the Naims' dispute. The marriage was annulled, and laws against mixed marriages prevailed.

Chief Justice Earl Warren was "furious," since he felt

that failing to take the case was "an evasion of the Court's responsibility."[10] The Chief Justice would have to wait for another opportunity to address issues involving interracial marriages. That chance came nine years later.

## McLaughlin v. Florida

In 1964, the United States Supreme Court had a chance to review a Florida law that made it illegal for interracial couples to live together without marrying. The Florida law ordered punishment for "any negro man and white woman, or any white man and negro woman, who are not married to each other, who shall . . . live in and occupy in the nighttime the same room."[11] No penalty was imposed for the same conduct by unmarried people of the same race.

The Court held that Florida's law violated the Equal Protection Clause of the Fourteenth Amendment. The state had to show an important enough reason for punishing a black person and a white person for conduct that was not punished when engaged in by members of the same race. If it could not, the racial classification contained in Florida's law "is reduced to an invidious discrimination forbidden by the Equal Protection Clause."[12] Despite its findings, the Supreme Court upheld the constitutionality of the law. However, it would be another three years before the Supreme Court had another opportunity to decide the issue of laws against intermarriage. That opportunity would be presented by Mildred and Richard Loving.

## Congress Helps the Civil Rights Movement

In addition to the earlier cases, the United States Supreme Court would also be required to evaluate the Lovings' case in light of federal laws. Only four years before Mildred and Richard Loving's case went before the Court, the civil rights movement in America had begun to gather energy. This movement was an effort to eliminate Jim Crow Laws, and to ensure that African Americans were treated equally under the law.

Dr. Martin Luther King, Jr., for example, led a campaign of nonviolence against segregation, the practice of keeping separate facilities for whites and nonwhites. Nightly television reports showed African-American protesters facing water cannons and police dogs in an effort to end the racist practices that kept them from enjoying all the rights and privileges of American citizenship.[13]

Other nonviolent means of protesting racial discrimination were the "lunch counter sit-ins." Throughout the country, many cafeterias and restaurants did not allow blacks to sit at the counter for service—these accommodations were strictly reserved for white patrons.

Martin Luther King, Jr., led the nonviolent protest movement against prejudice and segregation.

This form of discrimination was even practiced at the restaurant in the Georgia state capitol building. Several African-American students arranged a demonstration in protest. Ruby Doris Smith was among two hundred young people who passed along through the food line, making their selections. "[B]ut when we got to the cashier she wouldn't take our money . . . the Lieutenant-Governor came down and told us to leave. We didn't and went to the county jail."[14] Similar nonviolent civil rights demonstrations and protests took place throughout the United States.

African-American students from Saint Augustine College study while participating in a sit-in demonstration. Lunch counters were reserved for white customers only in this Raleigh, North Carolina, diner.

## Presidential Support

Finally, the efforts of the civil rights protesters made an impact on those at the highest levels of American government. President Lyndon B. Johnson challenged Congress to pass laws that would end segregation and other forms of discrimination against African Americans. Congress, as the legislative branch of the federal government, was charged with the responsibility of writing and passing federal laws.

In a speech before Congress on November 27, 1963, President Johnson said that

> (w)e have talked long enough in this country about equal rights. We have talked for a hundred years or more. It is time now to write the next chapter, and to write it in the books of law.[15]

Congress accepted the challenge, and the result was passage of the Civil Rights Act of 1964 and the Civil Rights Act of 1965.[16]

The Civil Rights Act of 1965 ended racial discrimination in voting. African Americans and other minorities no longer had to pass a reading test in order to be allowed to vote. The 1964 law made it illegal to discriminate against minorities in employment and public accommodations. African Americans who traveled for business or pleasure no longer had to suffer the

President Johnson (seated) is shown signing the Civil Rights Act of 1964. He is giving the pen he used to sign this historic law to Attorney General Robert Kennedy.

indignity of being denied a seat in a restaurant or lodging at hotels because of their race.

The stage had been set to eliminate the remaining traces of discrimination that were allowed by various state laws. The president had called for an end to racial discrimination, and the Supreme Court had struck down segregation and other forms of discrimination against African Americans. Congress passed sweeping laws that specifically outlawed certain forms of discrimination.

However, the Civil Rights Acts of 1964 and 1965 did leave many questions unanswered. For instance, could a state prevent an interracial couple from marrying? Since individual states typically determined their own laws regarding marriage, the fate of Richard and Mildred Loving seemed unclear. Only a favorable ruling from the Supreme Court of the United States could finally end the years of uncertainty.

# 4

# The Case for the Lovings

The time had come for Richard and Mildred Loving to present their case to the Supreme Court. They were represented by ACLU attorneys Bernard S. Cohen and Philip J. Hirschkop. As the two attorneys were preparing to appear before the Supreme Court, Richard Loving gave Cohen the following final instructions: "Tell the court that I love my wife, and it is just unfair that I can't live with her in Virginia."[1]

The defense attorneys' approach to arguing the Lovings' case seemed very simple. The Lovings' attorneys attacked all of Virginia's laws that affected interracial marriages. This approach fell into the following categories:

- by invalidating interracial marriages, the evasion law caused outrageous results;

- the evasion law and the law against interracial marriages were technically the same;

- the law against interracial marriage was a relic of slavery;

- Virginia's law caused great social harm;

- Virginia's law was discriminatory and denied equal protection; and

- Virginia's law violated due process.

## The Evasion Law Caused Outrageous Results

The evasion statute involved in the *Loving* case dealt with people who left Virginia to marry in another state and then returned to Virginia to live together as a married couple. According to Virginia law, couples who broke the evasion law were to be treated the same way as if the wedding had been performed within Virginia: both husband and wife would be subjected to criminal charges and the marriage would be considered void. Richard and Mildred Loving had been convicted under the evasion law. Attorneys Cohen and Hirschkop argued that this law caused outrageous results. One of the many problems a couple in an interracial marriage would face under this law was that one spouse might not be able to inherit the property of the other.

In one case, other heirs had prevented the surviving partner in a mixed marriage from inheriting the spouse's estate. Once the forbidden nature of the interracial marriage had been brought to the court's attention, the surviving spouse lost the right to inherit.[2]

The evasion law also created problems when a spouse in an interracial marriage died without a will. Virginia law provided that when a married person died without a will, that person's property would automatically become the property of the surviving spouse. Dying without a will is known as dying intestate. In such cases, Virginia courts make the decision that the surviving spouse receive a certain percentage of his or her deceased spouse's property. However, because Virginia did not recognize interracial marriages, the surviving spouse in such a marriage would not be able to inherit any of their deceased spouse's property. For couples like Richard and Mildred Loving, this result was unfair because it was based on the simple fact that they were of different races.

Mixed-race couples also lost benefits that other couples took for granted. For instance, during a worker's life, a certain portion of his or her paycheck is collected by the federal government and saved until the worker dies, retires, or is no longer able to work. At that time, monthly payments are made to the worker or the family to replace part of the income that was now lost. These payments are known as social security benefits. Interracial couples could not enjoy their spouse's social security benefits. This would be tragic for a man and woman who had lived together as husband and wife for many years. Even though they had loved and supported each other through the years, a husband or wife could not receive the benefits earned by their working spouse. Again, the only reason they could not receive those benefits was because the spouses were of different races.

Cohen and Hirschkop pointed out several other tragic results of the evasion law. The defense attorneys also noted that the Lovings, and other couples like them, could not file joint income tax returns because Virginia did not recognize them as a married couple. The attorneys went on to say that, legally, any children born to Richard and Mildred would be considered illegitimate.

For the same reason, Cohen and Hirschkop noted, in an interracial marriage, a husband could easily desert his wife and children. Since Virginia never recognized the marriage, it would not assume that the man was the father of the children. Therefore, the "husband" would

The front of Virginia's capitol building is shown here. It was in this building that restrictions against interracial marriages were written and passed into law. Fifteen other states also had laws prohibiting interracial marriages.

be under no *legal* obligation to support his wife and children.

Finally, married couples like Richard and Mildred Loving could be arrested and punished for living together without having been married. Although there are some couples who live together in a similar arrangement today, this was illegal in most cases when the Lovings were arrested in 1958. Even though Richard and Mildred Loving had been legally married in another state and publicly acknowledged their marriage, Virginia's laws said they were not married.

## Evasion Law Bans Interracial Marriage

Attorneys Cohen and Hirschkop also pointed out that the evasion law and Virginia's law against interracial marriage were technically the same. The evasion law punished interracial couples who left Virginia to marry legally in another state and then returned to Virginia to live there as a married couple. Virginia's law banning interracial marriages simply did not allow, or recognize, any marriage between people of different races.

Both laws were written to prevent interracial couples from marrying, so the Lovings' attorneys argued that the Supreme Court should consider Virginia's entire policy regarding interracial marriages. Because the Lovings had been convicted under the evasion law, it was possible that the Supreme Court might only find that portion of Virginia's law unconstitutional. But, if the Supreme Court failed to address Virginia's basic law against interracial marriages, Richard and Mildred Loving could later be arrested and jailed for the same act that led to their 1958 arrest.

Further, the defense attorneys pointed out, if Virginia's law against interracial marriages was found unconstitutional, there would be no constitutional reason to allow Virginia law to punish residents of Virginia who broke the evasion law. In other words, the two parts of Virginia's law were so closely tied together, they should both be reviewed by the Supreme Court.

In addition, Cohen and Hirschkop argued that the Lovings' eight-year marriage had always been in danger under Virginia law. Therefore, the Lovings would receive no justice if the Supreme Court did not also rule on the constitutionality of Virginia's basic law against mixed-race marriages. According to the attorneys, the miscegenation laws "rob the Negro race of its dignity, and only a decision which will reach the full body of these laws of the state of Virginia will change that."[3]

## Antimiscegenation Laws Are Relics of Slavery

Cohen and Hirschkop next argued that Virginia's antimiscegenation laws were the relics, or ancient

51

remains, of slavery, and expressions of racism. By imposing a ban on interracial marriages, Virginia branded African Americans as an inferior race. The defense attorneys quoted Professor Walter Wadlington who recalled Virginia's early history:

> It is surprising that Virginia which prides itself on the story of how one of her early white sons married an Indian princess today maintains one of the strictest statutory bans on racial intermarriage.[4]

Over the span of three centuries, Virginia passed many laws against interracial marriage—right up to 1932, when the most recent antimiscegenation laws were passed. The earlier laws against mixing the races were mostly for the purpose of protecting the slave owner's property rights over his slaves. The newer laws were mainly passed because of feelings of white racial superiority and a desire to preserve white "racial purity."

As proof that Virginia's laws prohibiting interracial marriages were a product of racist attitudes, Cohen and Hirschkop noted that the law against interracial marriage was entitled "Racial Integrity Act of 1924." In fact, the law was originally entitled "A Bill to Preserve the Integrity of the White Race."[5] It was clearly the attitude of the law's authors that white people were somehow superior to black people.

## Caste Systems and Nazis

Cohen and Hirschkop finished this section of their argument by informing the Supreme Court Justices that Virginia's law had been praised by a racist writer as "probably the most perfected expression of the white racial ideal since the institution of caste in India some 4000 years ago."[6] India's caste system was a rigid division of India's population into social class levels. The levels included the ruling class, the class of artists, a class for priests, and another class below all other classes, called the untouchables. This lowest class was required to perform all the tasks that the rest of Indian society considered too disgusting, or too lowly.

An Indian person was born into a particular class, and lived at that level of society for his or her entire life. No matter how hard a person worked, it was impossible for a member of any one of the lower classes to move into a higher class.

By noting this comparison of Virginia's law to India's ancient division of their society into classes, the defense attorneys may have been trying to show the Court how the separation of races in our nation was a part of our culture, stemming from the days of slavery. Another part of the defense team's point was that African Americans were seen as members of this country's lowest class. Similar to India's caste system, African

Americans were expected to remain in this class for their entire lives. Unless the Supreme Court addressed the problem, and found the antimiscegenation laws unconstitutional, the damaging attitudes would be even harder to root out in the coming decades.

Cohen and Hirschkop continued the comparison of Virginia's law to other historic divisions of society. The defense claimed that Virginia's law reminded one of "the laws of Nazi Germany."[7] During World War II, German officials investigated the background of the country's citizens to determine whether their family history included any members with Jewish blood.

Any individual with a particular amount of Jewish ancestry was classified as being Jewish. As we know, the Jews in Europe during World War II suffered terrible persecution and death at the hands of the Nazis. Cohen and Hirschkop pointed out similarities between Nazi Germany's government and Virginia's 1924 law. Both the Nazi government and Virginia's law separated the races, and took special care to determine the race of an individual, based on a ratio method.

Richard and Mildred Loving's attorneys noted that, under Virginia's then-current law, the state registrar of vital statistics was to prepare a form so that "persons could certify to their 'racial composition' to local registrars."[8] Deliberately including false information about color or race on that certificate was made a felony punishable by one year in prison.[9]

Marriage licenses were not to be issued unless the registrar was reasonably sure that the applicant's statements regarding their racial background were true. If the official doubted the racial makeup of the applicants, the "bride and groom" had to supply proof that they were telling the truth.

## Virginia's Law Causes Great Social Harm

Cohen and Hirschkop quoted American writer Thomas Pettigrew, who estimated that among African Americans the number with at least one known white ancestor was as high as 83 percent.[10] The defense attorneys noted that this high number of Americans with mixed blood was the result of the American slave system. During slavery, many white male slave owners impregnated their female slaves, resulting in racially mixed children.

Virginia's antimiscegenation laws could not reverse what had happened in the past or eliminate the proof that races had mixed during colonial times. Antimiscegenation laws could only attempt to prevent the further mixing of the races. Therefore, according to the defense team, the "ultimate evil" of these laws is that they inflict "an indignity upon every person . . .[seen] as not good enough to marry a white person."[11]

Finally, the Lovings' attorneys explained to the Court that supporters of Virginia's law simply used it to justify an entire system of discrimination. By pretending, perhaps sometimes even to themselves, that the true aim of Virginia's law was to keep the white race "pure," supporters were able to justify the true aim of this law—to keep the blacks in a lower place in society.[12] By focusing on the fear of intermarriage, whites did not have to openly demand a difference in social status between the two groups.

Cohen and Hirschkop named the antimiscegenation laws of Virginia and fifteen other states as the model of all the disabilities inflicted upon African Americans. Of the many laws that gave an inferior status to African Americans, it was also the last of this type of law to be addressed by the Supreme Court of the United States. As the most blatant, Cohen and Hirschkop urged the Court to strike down the miscegenation law, the "state's official symbol of a caste system."[13]

## Virginia's Law Denies Equal Protection

Another argument that the Lovings' attorneys presented to the United States Supreme Court was based on the constitutional guarantee of equal protection. The Fourteenth Amendment to the United States Constitution guarantees

Whether it was African-American women celebrating the fact that they no longer had to sit at the back of the bus (bottom right), or students protesting, desegregation prompted passionate responses throughout America.

equal protection under the law to all American citizens. Race should not be a factor in how people are treated in American courts.

In 1954, in *Brown* v. *Board of Education*, the United States Supreme Court struck down segregation in public schools as a violation of equal protection.[14] Thurgood Marshall, who successfully argued *Brown* v. *Board of Education* went on to become the first African-American Supreme Court Justice.

Cohen and Hirschkop argued that *Brown* meant that a state statute or law could not constitutionally deny blacks the freedom to associate with whites, or disadvantage black people by any form of segregation. The Lovings' attorneys claimed that the reasoning behind *Brown* should also mean that miscegenation laws denied equal protection to Virginia's African-American citizens.[15]

In fact, Cohen and Hirschkop argued, Virginia's antimiscegenation laws seemed more clearly unconstitutional than school segregation for the following reasons:

• The right of two consenting adults to marry each other seems even more basic than the right of students to attend a racially mixed school.

• Where students may choose to attend a private school that offers a racially mixed student body

Thurgood Marshall (center) is shown after the Supreme Court announced its landmark decision in *Brown* v. *Board of Education* in 1954. Marshall went on to become the first African-American Supreme Court Justice.

as an alternative to public school, a mixed couple who wish to marry clearly have no other alternative.

- Both parties in a mixed marriage wish to associate, or join together as husband and wife. In *Brown*, however, at least some of the white students did not wish to associate with the black students.

The attorneys for the Lovings then addressed the problem of the upholding of miscegenation laws in *Pace v. Alabama*. This previous Supreme Court decision held that the laws did not discriminate against African Americans. After all, since the prohibition against intermarriage applied equally to both blacks and whites, the Supreme Court had concluded that the law applied equally to all races.[16] Cohen and Hirschkop pointed out that this theory took a limited view of the Fourteenth Amendment. This amendment was supposed to eliminate all forms of discrimination based on race.[17]

Cohen and Hirschkop argued that state laws that discriminated against any one race had been struck down in many other cases. These examples involved rights much less important than the right to marry, including:

- the need for information about race in voting and property records;[18]

• the need for information about race on nomination papers and ballots; and[19]

• segregation in public parks and playgrounds.[20]

The Lovings' attorneys reminded the Supreme Court of another decision that seemed to end the matter of race-based discrimination. In *Hirabayashi* v. *United States* in 1943, the Supreme Court upheld a race-based category. However, in that decision, the Supreme Court of the United States held that

> [d]istinctions between citizens solely because of their ancestry are by their very nature odious to a free people whose institutions are founded upon the doctrine of equality. For that reason, legislative classification or discrimination based on race alone has often been held to be a denial of equal protection.[21]

In fact, the Lovings' attorneys argued to the Court, the purpose of the Fourteenth Amendment was to root out racial discrimination, from official sources, among the individual states. State laws that outlawed intermarriage certainly fell within this category, since there is no constitutionally proper basis for preventing such marriages. Maintaining racial purity or pride might appear to some to be a proper or desirable goal, but it was truly nothing more than a device to "cloak ignorance."[22]

The guarantee of equal protection does not allow the government to take rights away from any racial

Robert Kennedy visited Coretta Scott King at her home after her husband, Martin Luther King, Jr., was assassinated.

group. The Lovings' attorneys claimed that the desire to maintain racial purity was not a proper, or important enough, reason to give unequal treatment to different races. According to Cohen and Hirschkop, those goals had no "overriding statutory purpose" that would justify denial of equal protection under the law.

Finally, Cohen and Hirschkop argued that even if racial purity were an acceptable purpose under the Constitution, Virginia's law was not designed to achieve that result.

> The only race kept 'pure' is the Caucasian. This is because the Virginia laws are not designed to preserve the purity of races but . . . only the integrity of members of . . . the so-called 'White' or Anglo-Saxon race.[23]

Cohen and Hirschkop noted that a marriage between a person of Chinese ancestry and a "colored person" would not be illegal under Virginia's law. If Virginia's lawmakers truly wanted to keep the races "pure," then it would be just as important to keep the African-American, Chinese, and American Indian races pure. Certainly, the defense attorneys pointed out, failing to protect racial purity of the other races is not equal protection.[24] Essentially, Virginia's concept of race was nothing more than a "combination of legal fiction and genetic nonsense."[25] The law was designed to preserve the social status of Virginia's largest and most powerful group.

The only other purpose of Virginia's miscegenation law was to prevent "corruption of the blood" from racial intermixing, which would "weaken or destroy the quality of" Virginia's citizens.[26] Cohen and Hirschkop argued that this reason was not good enough to justify discrimination among Virginia's citizens. Furthermore, the attorneys pointed out, there was no reputable scientific evidence to prove that a person of mixed blood was "somehow inferior in quality to one of racial purity. . . ."[27]

In the end, Virginia's laws were nothing more than relics of slavery, Cohen and Hirschkop argued. There was no constitutional justification for the law against intermarriage. The miscegenation laws had been passed at first as part of the institution of slavery. They reappeared in their present form as part of the racial antagonism and intolerance that has marked our country's history.

The Lovings' lawyers then turned to their most powerful arguments against Virginia's laws—the Fourteenth Amendment to the United States Constitution.

## Virginia's Law Violates the Due Process Clause

The Fourteenth Amendment promises American citizens due process of law. Due process requires, among other things, that rules be followed during the course of each trial in order to protect the rights and freedoms of those involved in the case. This means that, before anyone's property or freedom can be taken away, the government must take special steps.

In the case of the Lovings, this would mean some kind of trial or hearing was required before the state of Virginia could decide that Richard and Mildred Loving could not marry. The Lovings did have a trial before they were sentenced for breaking Virginia's law against miscegenation. However, their basic freedom to marry without interference from the state of Virginia was taken away without any kind of trial or hearing. The fact that this freedom was denied was a denial of due process, according to Cohen and Hirschkop.

The attorneys reminded the Supreme Court that "marriage is perhaps the most important and most personal of all human relationships."[28] Therefore, marriage was one of the freedoms that was protected by the Due Process Clause of the Fourteenth Amendment.

## Reasonable Limits on the Right to Marry

The Lovings' attorneys recognized that the right to marry was not an absolute right. There were legitimate government reasons for restricting marriage in certain circumstances. For instance, Virginia could impose reasonable age and health limitations on the right to marry. These limitations would protect the population of Virginia from the results of marrying too young. The state could also prohibit polygamous marriage, which is the marriage of an individual to more than one partner. In this case, the restriction would protect society from the deterioration of the family unit.

However, Cohen and Hirschkop argued, Virginia's antimiscegenation law had no legitimate government objective. The enforcement of such a law would deprive the Lovings, without due process of law, of their right to marry. Virginia's law had nothing to do with the preservation of health or the family unit. The law simply supported the myth that blacks were by nature inferior to whites.

At the end of their brief, Cohen and Hirschkop challenged the Supreme Court of the United States:

> there are no laws more symbolic of the Negro's delegation to second class citizenship. Whether or not this Court has been wise to avoid this issue in the past, the time has come to strike down these laws; they are legalized racial prejudice, unsupported by reason or morals, and should not exist in good society.[29]

Had the time truly come for the Supreme Court to strike down antimiscegenation laws? Bernard Cohen and Philip Hirschkop had placed their blunt request before the Court on behalf of the Lovings.

While the Supreme Court considered Richard and Mildred Loving's appeal, it was also able to review several points raised by a number of individuals and large groups who supported the Lovings and who had put their opinions in writing. These supporters offered a document, known as a brief, to the Supreme Court. The individuals and groups were called *amicus curiae* (which means "friend of the court" in Latin).

## Catholic Bishops Support the Lovings

The Roman Catholic supporters included bishops and archbishops from such places as Richmond, Atlanta, New Orleans, San Antonio, Charleston, and Baltimore, just to name a few. The National Catholic Conference for Interracial Justice and the National Catholic Social Action Conference also contributed to the brief submitted to the Supreme Court.

The brief included issues that had not been argued by the Lovings' attorneys. The Catholic bishops' brief pointed out that "religion does not pertain to the mind alone; it involves the whole person."[30] According to the bishops, "marriage is a fundamental act of religion, and, because of this, marriage comes within the constitutionally protected 'free exercise of religion.'"[31]

The Catholic bishops' *amicus* brief did acknowledge the fact that marriage was always controlled, to a certain extent, by state lawmakers. However, that did not mean that state lawmakers had complete control over the subject of marriage. The Catholic bishops reminded the Court that marriage was an exercise of religion. The First Amendment of the Constitution protects a person's expression of his or her religion without any government interference. Therefore, a marriage, as a religious expression, would be protected, and as such, fell within the First Amendment freedoms. An earlier Supreme Court decision held that First Amendment freedoms could be restricted only to prevent grave and immediate danger to interests that the state may lawfully protect.[32] Therefore, it would be proper for Virginia to write some laws that affected marriage.

In addition to points mentioned in Cohen and Hirschkop's brief, the bishops' brief also mentioned the age at which people may marry, the proper procedure to make a legal marriage, and the duties and obligations created by marriage. According to the Catholic bishops' brief, the failure of the state to make laws addressing these issues would create serious problems that Virginia would properly wish to avoid. However, none of those proper regulations were connected in any way to the issues that the antimiscegenation statutes were created to avoid.[33]

Next, the Catholic bishops' brief addressed the very nature of marriage.

[M]arriage is much more than a social event or the commencement of a social relationship . . . [It] is held by the major religious faiths in the United States to be an important act of religion. Marriage is so important as an act of faith that several religious faiths in the United States specifically did not allow any restriction on marriages because of race.

The Catholic bishops also relied on a Catholic legal scholar who wrote about miscegenation laws in 1843. He said that even though interracial marriages may not be legal under a state's law, they are valid under church law. "If some wish to enter such a marriage, they cannot be forbidden the sacraments because of a legal prohibition or public opinion since they are exercising a natural right" that the Church allows.[34]

## Suffering Caused By Outsiders To The Marriage

The bishops' brief noted that interracial families may suffer, but this is not because of anything in the family structure or in the marriage. Instead, it is due to the lack of understanding and race prejudice that interracial families encounter. According to the bishops, this suffering comes from people outside the immediate family. Therefore, any of the reasons that make restrictions on marriage appropriate do not answer any of the problems raised by interracial marriage.

The Catholic bishops also argued to the Supreme Court that the right to have children was recognized as a fundamental human right. Since Virginia's laws outlawed marriage between people of different races, those laws were unconstitutional because they denied these families the right to have children.[35]

Virginia's laws make race the test of whether a man and woman may marry. For that reason, those who could not pass this racial test were kept from one of the chief lawful rights in marriage—having children.[36] The Catholic bishops concluded that the difference between those who may marry and lawfully have children and those who may not, is based solely on race. Those who wished to marry outside their own race received different treatment under the law. Therefore, Virginia's laws violated the Equal Protection Clause of the Fourteenth Amendment.

## Japanese Americans Address the Court

In addition to the Catholic bishops and archbishops, the Lovings also had the support of the Japanese American Citizens League (JACL). This group of Japanese American citizens fought for equal rights for its members. Since a number of states had laws that prohibited people of Japanese ancestry from marrying whites, the JACL was interested in the outcome of the Lovings' case.

Attorney William Marutani also prepared an *amicus* brief on behalf of the JACL and submitted it to the Court. Marutani recalled first the large number of invasions and cross-invasions throughout Europe over the centuries. This would make it difficult, if not impossible, for white people to prove that they had no trace whatever of any blood other than Caucasian.

Further, the JACL attorney informed the Supreme Court that scientists had flatly rejected the concept of a "pure" race. Nevertheless, clerks in town halls throughout Virginia had the power to determine whether a marriage applicant was of "pure white race." Marutani was troubled by the idea that these clerks had the responsibility of interpreting such terms as "colored person," "white person," or "Caucasian." Since their interpretation could result in criminal penalties, it was wrong for Virginia to use such vague terms.

The United States Constitution requires state laws to be precise. If they are not, the state law can be struck down by the Supreme Court for being too vague. It was Marutani's argument that Virginia's law should be struck down by the Supreme Court for that very reason.[37]

The Lovings had presented their arguments to the Supreme Court. Their position was supported by briefs from a large segment of the Roman Catholic Church's clergy in America, the Japanese American Citizens League, and other groups. Each brief contained strong arguments in favor of striking down Virginia's law. However, the Supreme Court could not yet make a decision. The Court still had to hear arguments on the other side of the case, from the state of Virginia.

# 5

# The Case for Virginia

The Commonwealth of Virginia also had an opportunity to submit its arguments to the Supreme Court in a brief. The Supreme Court of Appeals of Virginia had upheld the state's antimiscegenation law. It fell to Robert Y. Button, as attorney general of Virginia, to guide the team that would prepare the brief that Virginia would present to the Justices of the United States Supreme Court. He was assisted in his task by Kenneth C. Patty and R. D. McIlwaine, III, both assistant attorneys general. The arguments presented by the Commonwealth of Virginia fell into the following simple categories:

• The only portion of Virginia's law under attack was the evasion statute;

- The Fourteenth Amendment was not meant to interfere with the power of the individual states to outlaw interracial marriages;

- The state had very good reasons for outlawing interracial marriages; and

- Laws about marriage should be left to the individual states to control.

## Evasion Law Under Attack

Button, McIlwaine, and Patty first argued that the only portion of the antimiscegenation statute that the Supreme Court should consider was the evasion part of the law. That was the section of Virginia's law that made it a crime to leave the state to marry and then return to Virginia to live there as husband and wife. The Supreme Court of Appeals of Virginia had considered only that portion of Virginia's law and had found it to be valid. The Supreme Court of Appeals of Virginia did not make any decision about Virginia's law that declared mixed marriages to be void.

According to Virginia's attorneys, this meant that the Supreme Court of the United States should only consider the evasion portion of the law. Since no Virginia official had brought the question of the Lovings' marital status into question, then the Court

74

should not consider that matter. If the lawyers for Virginia convinced the Supreme Court of this point, the Court could make a decision about the evasion law. But, even if the evasion law was struck down, the law that said the Lovings' marriage was a "nonmarriage" would still stand. In that case, it might be many more years before a case similar to the Lovings' came before the Supreme Court for consideration. Until that time, marriages like the Lovings could be considered void in Virginia and fifteen other states.

## Miscegenation Laws Not Affected by Fourteenth Amendment

Virginia's team of lawyers argued that the state's code did not violate the Fourteenth Amendment to the United States Constitution. The brief written for the Commonwealth of Virginia included a great deal of information about the debates in Congress when the Fourteenth Amendment was being considered for adoption. McIlwaine's brief noted that "the prime effort . . . in construing a constitutional provision, is to . . . give effect to the intent of the framers and of the people who adopted it."[1] This idea suggests a certain method for interpreting the law: In order to understand what the Fourteenth Amendment means, judges should look at what the writers of the law meant to accomplish.

The attorneys for Virginia researched the debates over earlier civil rights laws in order to determine the meaning of the Fourteenth Amendment. The state's attorneys then gave examples to show what the framers of the Fourteenth Amendment intended to do by passing that amendment. One example was that of Senator Thomas A. Hendricks of Indiana. The senator opposed passage of the Civil Rights Act of 1866, the forerunner to the Fourteenth Amendment.

Hendricks feared that the civil rights that would be granted by the Civil Rights Act would abolish many of Indiana's laws. One such law was an "Indiana constitutional provision which provided that no Negro man should be allowed to intermarry with a white woman."[2] Hendricks was troubled by the idea that Indiana laws would be "disregarded" because of the new federal law.[3]

Virginia's brief included the opinion of Senator Lyman Trumbull of Illinois, who had introduced the Civil Rights Bill. Senator Trumbull made it clear that there was no intention to "nullify the anti-miscegenation statutes . . . of the various states." He even went so far as to tell opponents of the bill that "it is a misrepresentation of this bill to say that it interferes with [antimiscegenation] laws."[4] The new civil rights law was passed only to make sure that the same punishment was dealt out to people of "every race and color."[5]

The purpose of the Fourteenth Amendment was to give power to Congress to pass laws similar to the Civil Rights Act. The difference between the Civil Rights Act and the amendment was that the Civil Rights Act could be repealed by a majority of Congress. If the unjust laws of some of the states were to be struck down, the strength of the United States Constitution and its amendments could be used.[6] However, the unjust laws that were the targets of the Civil Rights Act, and therefore, the Fourteenth Amendment, were only those laws that allowed blacks to be punished more harshly than whites.

Nothing in the Fourteenth Amendment specifically allows federal laws to interfere with the antimiscegenation laws of the individual states. Those who wrote and adopted that amendment did not intend for the Fourteenth Amendment to have that effect. The legal team for Virginia declared that, if "nothing new can be put into the Constitution except through the [amendment] process," the present attack on the Virginia statutes must fail.[7]

## Judicial Legislation

Button, McIlwaine, and Patty also reminded the Supreme Court that it would be inappropriate for the Court to question the wisdom of the state policy that prevented interracial marriages. Such an action on the part of the Supreme Court would be judicial legislation. If the United States Supreme Court considered scientific evidence, and made a decision based on that evidence, this would amount to law-making by the Court. Since law-making is strictly the responsibility of Congress, the Court would be intruding on Congress's area of power.

According to Virginia's attorneys, even if the Court did make such an inquiry, it would "quickly find itself mired in a . . . bog of conflicting scientific opinion upon the effects of interracial marriage. . . ."[8] Virginia's attorneys quoted a number of "experts" from earlier cases. Those quotes demonstrated that opinions on interracial marriage could be quite diverse.

In the opinion of some experts, racial intermarriages have sometimes produced a better race.[9] However, other experts warned that, in interracial marriages, the inferior qualities of one race are not "bred out", but may be emphasized in their children.[10] Researchers also claimed that there were higher rates of divorce among the intermarried, since greater stress and strain is put upon the marriage than is true for other marriages.[11] Also, some experts pointed to the fact that people identify with certain groups. Group identity affects many aspects of ordinary daily life, making mixed marriages more difficult than non-mixed marriages.

Obviously, there were many different opinions on the subject of interracial marriage. According to the state of Virginia, there was certainly enough evidence to support the claim that it was in the best interest of its citizens to prevent interracial marriages. The attorneys for Virginia argued that it is entirely up to the lawmakers of each individual state to decide what is best for its citizens. These lawmakers were capable of developing a policy of permitting or preventing interracial marriage. They could also take responsibility for evaluating the opinions of experts on the subject of interracial marriage. The Supreme Court should, therefore, not consider any scientific evidence regarding interracial marriage.

## A Matter for the States to Decide

Under the United States Constitution, the regulation and control of traditional state matters, including marriage and family relationships, are reserved to the states. Regulating who may marry, and under what circumstances, involves the exercise of one of the most important powers of the individual states.

Concluding their arguments, Button, Patty, and McIlwaine reminded the Supreme Court that the

Chief Justice Earl Warren's desire to see equal rights for all races made some Americans oppose him. This sign in Appleton, Wisconsin, demands that Warren be removed from the Supreme Court. Because the sign was put up without a permit, however, it had to be removed.

Virginia laws under attack reflected a policy that had been in effect in Virginia for over two centuries. Also, the same policy was still the law in fifteen other states.

Considering this history, the Supreme Court should not find that the laws in question violated the constitutional rights of the Lovings. In earlier cases, the Supreme Court had upheld such laws. McIlwaine and the other lawyers for Virginia claimed that it was difficult to understand how any other conclusion could be reached.

> Marriage, as creating the most important relation in life, as having more to do with the morals and civilization of a people than any other institution, has always been subject to the control of the Legislature.[12]

The lawyers for Virginia finished their brief by asking the Supreme Court of the United States to affirm the judgment of the Supreme Court of Appeals of Virginia. Just as the Lovings had the support of several groups, Virginia also was not alone in its position. Virginia's attorneys found support from another state, one with its own antimiscegenation law.

## North Carolina Supports Virginia

Virginia received support from the state of North Carolina in the form of an *amicus curiae* brief prepared by T. W. Bruton, attorney general of that state. North

Carolina presented its arguments to the Supreme Court because it was interested in the outcome of Virginia's case. If Virginia's law was found unconstitutional, then North Carolina's law against miscegenation could also be struck down as unconstitutional.

Bruton's brief showed little, if any, restraint. The language of North Carolina's *amicus* brief revealed the writer's distaste for interracial marriages. The brief also hinted at the anger created by the idea of the Supreme Court meddling in state matters.

North Carolina did not limit its opposition to interracial marriages by simply passing a law against the practice. The restriction appeared in the state constitution. Article 14, Section 8, of the constitution of North Carolina provided that: "All marriages between a white person and a Negro, or between a white person and a person of Negro descent to the third generation, inclusive, are hereby forever prohibited."[13] North Carolina obviously felt so strongly that interracial marriages should be prevented that it made the prohibition part of its state constitution.

Like Virginia, North Carolina pointed to the original understanding of the Fourteenth Amendment. North Carolina argued that unless the Fourteenth Amendment was supposed to be a license for federal courts to "sink every state ship in sight if they do not like the cut of its sails," then Virginia's historic position was clearly sound.[14]

North Carolina's argument was simply that federal courts, including the Supreme Court, were not allowed to strike down laws simply because they did not find those laws appealing. Bruton wrote that Virginia's position was especially correct, considering that the states that voted to pass the Fourteenth Amendment did not think they were striking down their own laws against interracial marriages.[15]

In its brief, North Carolina agreed with Virginia's argument that there were conflicting opinions about the effects of interracial marriages. According to North Carolina's brief, there is no "concrete exactness in this field."[16] Only one claim could be proven: that none of the existing scientific information could ever settle the question as to whether or not interracial marriage would be harmful to the state.

Since that was the case, North Carolina's brief concluded that it was up to each state to decide what was best for its citizens.

> If the State feels like the life of its people is better protected by a policy of racial integrity . . . then it has the right to legislate in such a field. The fact that the state's conclusions may differ from the conclusions of other groups should not affect the matter unless minority

83

groups are entitled to . . . privileges that are against the judgment of the majority.[17]

## The Supreme Court Considers the Case

The arguments of both sides had been presented to the Supreme Court. It was now up to the highest Court in the land to judge the merits of the arguments, and to determine which side was supported by the United States Constitution. Would the Court uphold the "right" of the individual states to determine who a person may marry and who he or she may not marry? Or, would the Supreme Court uphold the right of an individual to marry as he or she pleased?

The Lovings and the state of Virginia all felt that their opinions were supported by the United States Constitution. How would the Court rule? The attorneys on both sides of the case had looked at the Supreme Court history on cases involving civil rights, and at the histories of the individual Supreme Court Justices. By doing so, they hoped to predict the outcome of their own cases.

# 6

# The Supreme Court's Decision

The state of Virginia and the Lovings' attorneys had each presented their case in writing to the Supreme Court—in written briefs and in oral arguments. After the oral arguments, the Justices retired to consider the arguments and to come to a final decision.

This process can take up to several months. First, the nine Justices meet to discuss the case. During the discussions, no one other than the Justices is allowed in the meeting room. When the discussions are over, each Justice writes his or her own opinion and then delivers a copy of it to the other eight Justices. They all then meet again to vote on the outcome of the case. The Chief Justice of the Supreme Court appoints one of the other Justices to write the majority opinion. This opinion—held by more than half of the Justices—determines which side "wins" in the case.

On June 12, 1967, the Supreme Court came to a unanimous decision. All nine Justices agreed on the outcome of the Lovings' appeal. Chief Justice Earl Warren delivered the opinion of the Court. The Court held that Virginia had violated the United States Constitution by preventing marriages between people of different races.[1]

The Supreme Court rejected the idea that equal application under the law was only required when the issue was equal punishment for the same crime, regardless of race. Therefore, Chief Justice Warren wrote, the Court did not accept the state's argument that the laws should be upheld if there was any possible reason to decide that they serve a rational purpose.[2] The Fourteenth Amendment placed a "very heavy burden of justification" for any state statute, or law, that includes classifications based on race.

Chief Justice Warren then responded bluntly to Virginia's case. There could be "no question but that Virginia's miscegenation statutes rest solely upon distinctions drawn according to race. The statutes proscribe generally accepted conduct engaged in by members of different races."[3]

Next, the Warren Court addressed Virginia's argument that the framers of the Fourteenth Amendment did not intend for antimiscegenation statutes to be affected by the new amendment. The Chief Justice agreed that such historical research could sometimes assist judges in interpreting a particular law. However, those sources could only shed *some* light on the interpretation of the Fourteenth Amendment. They were not sufficient to resolve the question faced by the Supreme Court.[4]

Chief Justice Warren agreed that those who supported post-Civil War amendments meant to improve the status of the freed slaves. The framers intended the Fourteenth Amendment to remove all legal differences among American citizens. At the same time, Warren wrote, those who opposed passage of the Fourteenth Amendment were "antagonistic to both the letter and the spirit of the Amendments and wished them to have the most limited effect."[5]

Next, the Supreme Court addressed Virginia's argument that earlier Supreme Court decisions supported their "equal application" theory. Chief Justice Warren explained simply, that the earlier Supreme Court decisions represented "a limited view of the Equal Protection Clause which has not withstood analysis in the subsequent decisions of this court."[6] In recent years, the Supreme Court had had other opportunities to evaluate the Fourteenth Amendment and had come to a different conclusion.

Chief Justice Warren wrote that making distinctions between citizens based solely on race was "odious to free people whose institutions are founded upon the doctrine of equality."[7] According to Chief Justice Warren, the fact that Virginia only prohibited interracial marriages between white people and people of color (not between two people of color) showed that the race classification was designed to maintain white supremacy.[8]

The Supreme Court held that there was no doubt that "restricting the freedom to marry solely because of racial classifications violates the central meaning of the Equal Protection Clause."[9]

## Virginia's Law Violates Due Process

The Supreme Court also decided that Virginia's law deprived Richard and Mildred Loving of liberty without due process of law. That deprivation violated the Due Process Clause of the Fourteenth Amendment. Chief Justice Warren wrote that marriage was one of the "basic civil rights of man."[10] Denial of that fundamental freedom based on race went against the very principal of equality at the heart of the Fourteenth Amendment.

Chief Justice Warren closed his opinion for the Court with this very specific language:

> The Fourteenth Amendment requires that the freedom of choice to marry not be restricted by invidious racial discriminations. Under our Constitution, the freedom to marry, or not marry, a person of another race resides with the individual and cannot be infringed by the State. These convictions must be reversed. It is so ordered.[11]

## Victory for the Lovings

The long years of waiting were finally over for Mildred and Richard Loving and their three children. Just ten days after their ninth wedding anniversary, the Supreme Court struck down the Virginia law that made it illegal for the Lovings to live together as husband and wife in their home state.

With the law overturned and their convictions reversed, the Lovings could no longer be considered felons under Virginia law. Nothing, however, could ever make up for the time Mildred and Richard Loving had spent away from their families, or the insult of being banished from Virginia for living together there "against the peace and dignity" of the state.

Both Richard and Mildred Loving felt relief after the Supreme Court handed down its decision. Richard said that, "[I]t was a great burden. . . . It's hard to believe.

Now I can put my arm around my wife in Virginia."[12] Unfortunately, not everyone felt that justice had been done. Sheriff Garnett Brooks, the man who had arrested the Lovings in their home nine years earlier, said he was from the old school. "I still think the law should be on the books."[13]

Surprisingly, neither Richard nor Mildred Loving had set out to make great changes in constitutional law. According to attorney Bernard Cohen, the Lovings were "uncomplicated people who were not interested in making a statement or becoming civil-rights heroes."[14] However, this young couple had changed the law, simply because they loved each other, and were not willing to allow an unjust law to interfere with their basic right to marry the person of their choice.

# 7

# The Impact of the Loving Decision

Supreme Court decisions are obviously important to the participants who bring their case before the country's highest court. However, the Supreme Court has its greatest impact on American society when the laws we live by are changed.

Did the *Loving* decision change American life as other Supreme Court decisions had done in the past? Look at the way life in America was described in the early chapters of this book. Compare those descriptions to the attitudes of today. Consider your own feelings on the subject of interracial marriage. Then, decide for yourself if the *Loving* case helped to change attitudes among Americans.

It is difficult to tell, even more than thirty years after the decision on *Loving* was announced, whether Americans have changed their minds about interracial marriage. In 1967, the same year *Loving* was announced, Americans still seemed uncomfortable, at best, with the idea of intermarriage. That same year, Secretary of State Dean Rusk's daughter Peggy, married Guy Smith, an African American. The headline in *The New York Times* announced the event: "Rusk's Daughter, 18, Is Wed to Negro."[1] It is significant that the story appeared on the front page of *The New York Times*, rather than in the society section, along with other wedding announcements. It is just as noteworthy that the groom was referred to simply as "a Negro," rather than by his name.

The *Times*'s attention to the marriage probably reflected the shock that many Americans felt when forced to confront interracial marriages. Dean Rusk himself appeared to believe that Americans would not accept the marriage. Concerned that it might embarrass Lyndon Johnson, the president at that time, Rusk offered to resign if the president thought it was necessary.[2]

Apparently, President Johnson did not take Rusk's offer to resign seriously, because the offer was neither accepted nor denied.[3] Many Americans did disapprove of the marriage, however. One California man claimed that "I'd probably kill any of my children before I'd let them do such a thing."[4]

Little more than ten years later, it became evident that relationships between whites and blacks were still unacceptable to many Americans. In 1980, Joseph Paul Franklin shot and killed two young black men who were jogging together with two white women in a Salt Lake City park.[5] Franklin publicly admitted to the murders; he explained that "it was just because they were race mixing."[6] As a member of the Ku Klux Klan, Franklin opposed interracial dating or marriage. "Had they not been race mixing, you know, it would have been a totally different story."[7] Franklin received a life sentence for the murders.

As recently as 1996, even some school officials sometimes displayed an intolerant and racist attitude toward racial mixing. In that year, an Alabama high school principal said that interracial couples would not be allowed at the school prom. One student, the daughter of an interracial couple, asked the principal why he had made that rule. He responded that the rule was meant to prevent "mistakes" like her.[8] The principal was quickly removed from his job, and all couples were allowed to attend the prom. The comment, however, was not soon forgotten.

However, times may be changing. Today, mixed marriages are even more common than before. Many black celebrities have white spouses. Among these are basketball player Charles Barkley, actor Cuba Gooding, Jr., television personality Montel Williams, and model Iman. Their marriages scarcely receive comment.

As interracial couples today know, rude reactions still happen, but they are generally the exception rather than the rule. Younger people seem to put far less focus on racial boundaries.[9] Debra Vaughn believes that reactions to her mixed marriage have been "more positive than negative. Sometimes, a person's first look when we walk into a store, whatever that look is, is completely changed by the time we leave there. People really seem to enjoy us [as a couple.]"[10]

Seventy-five percent of a group of interracial couples in a study reported that they still had very positive relationships with their parents.[11] Also since the *Loving* decision, marriages between blacks and whites have jumped 378 percent between 1970 and 1992. This is from about sixty-five thousand interracial couples to some two hundred forty-six thousand, an additional 181,000 such marriages.[12]

## Moving Forward

Interracial couples may also be finding support from people outside their families. In November 1998, South Carolina voters agreed to remove the ban on interracial

These students are picketing against segregation. It was nonviolent demonstrations like this one that paved the way for equal rights among all Americans.

marriages that had been included in the state's constitution when it was written in 1895. Even though the *Loving* decision took away any legal effect that the South Carolina law may have had, the voters wanted to demonstrate their disapproval of the law.[13]

Similar action was being discussed in Alabama late in 1998. That state's constitution, enacted in 1910, forbids marriages between any white person and a black person or a descendant of a black person. Although Alabama's law also lacks force of law, Auburn University professor Wayne Flynt said that black lawmakers were "eager to remove a symbol of racism."[14]

Despite many positive strides, interracial couples account for fewer than one percent of all married couples in America.[15] Obviously, we still live in a society where love is not always "color blind." The extended families of interracial couples worry about the way their loved ones will be accepted in their community. Often, the parents of partners in mixed marriages are also concerned about the difficulties their grandchildren would have in society.[16]

Love may not conquer all, but in Richard and Mildred Loving's case, it did conquer a law that was one of many legal barriers that kept people of different races from coming to know each other.

# Questions for Discussion

1. Look at Virginia's law regarding interracial marriages that was in effect at the time the Lovings were arrested. Go to an encyclopedia and look up and read the story of John Rolfe and Pocahantas. Make special note of where they lived in the American colonies. If John Rolfe and Pocahantas were to marry in Virginia at the time the Lovings were arrested, would they have been in violation of Virginia's antimiscegenation law?

2. Why was intermarriage outlawed during Colonial times? Why was intermarriage outlawed during the Lovings' time? What accounts for the changes, if any, in the reasons for these laws?

3. The Supreme Court's unanimous decision declaring that laws against intermarriage were unconstitutional was directed to Virginia's particular laws. Does that mean that the remaining states with antimiscegenation laws were not required to repeal those laws? Or, did the *Loving* decision end such laws in all states? Divide the class into two groups. One group should list any reasons it has for believing that the *Loving* decision ended laws

against intermarriage. The other group should list any reasons it has for believing the decision did not end such laws. Discuss your findings with the rest of the class.

4. Individual states decide the rules as to who may marry and under what circumstances. These laws usually cover such concerns as the age of the bride and groom, their health, and whether either is already a partner in an existing marriage. Discuss the reasons for these laws. Next, list any reasons for, or against, interracial marriages. Discuss the differences, if any, between the two separate lists.

5. Catholic bishops and other groups supported the Lovings' struggle to strike down the antimiscegenation law. Can you think of any other groups that exist now that might also have supported the Lovings? What reasons might these groups have for doing so? Write a list of the arguments such groups might make.

6. Divide the class equally among the number of groups listed in response to question 5. Nine students should be selected to serve as your "Supreme Court." Pretend that each of the groups is the legal team for each of the organizations listed. Using the list of arguments you prepared for question 5, prepare a legal brief that presents your arguments to the "Supreme Court." Your briefs should only be a few pages long, but they should also thoroughly explain your arguments.

Each group should select one "attorney" who will make the group's presentation before the Court. This is known as the oral argument. Take fifteen minutes for each group to make its argument before the Court. Be prepared for questions from the "Supreme Court Justices," who may interrupt to ask questions.

This is different from a true oral argument before the Supreme Court, when attorneys for the opposing side would also be giving their arguments. The object of this exercise is just to give you a chance to develop your own arguments, and to write your own brief.

When all the groups have made their presentations, the nine Supreme Court Justices should discuss the briefs and then vote. After the decision is made, the Justices should prepare a written opinion, giving their reasons for deciding as they did. Finally, have one "Justice" announce the Court's decision to the class.

7. As a member of the class, approach a married couple you know well. Explain to the couple that you are working on a class project. Ask them to pretend that there is a state law that makes their marriage illegal, and in fact, has legally ended their marriage. They have no right to appeal this law, and they will be arrested if they stay together. You may have to invent a "law" to explain why their marriage is "illegal." For instance, they may be of different religions, ethnic backgrounds, or, as in the case of the Lovings, members of different races. Act as though you are a reporter. Take notes of their reactions and statements. Ask them the following questions:

- What do you think of such a law?

- Will you fight this law, and if so, how?

- Who will you turn to for help?

- Why do you think this law is wrong?

- Do you think the state has the right to decide who a person may marry, and who he or she may not marry?

After you finish interviewing the married couple, share the Lovings' story with them. Ask them if they were aware that as recently as 1967, fifteen states had laws against interracial marriages. Then, each student should discuss his or her findings with the class. Discuss the similarities or differences between your couple's reactions and arguments, and those made by the Lovings and their attorneys.

8. Examine your own feelings on the subject of interracial marriages. Are you surprised or offended when you see a "mixed" couple? For many people, the sight of an interracial couple can bring up strong feelings. Religion, culture, power, and morality all play a part in the way we see these relationships. What do you think accounts for your feelings on the subject? You may not even have strong feelings on the issue either way. However, sometimes remaining silent on a subject speaks loudest of all. Others may assume that your silence means support for their position.

# Chapter Notes

## Introduction
1. *Loving* v. *Virginia* 388 U.S. 1, 3 (1967), Record.
2. Peter Irons and Stephanie Guitton, eds., *May It Please the Court* (New York: The New Press, 1993), p. 278.
3. "Anti-Miscegenation Statutes: Repugnant Indeed," *Time*, July 23, 1967, p. 45.

## Chapter 1. Laws Against Interracial Marriage
1. *Loving* v. *Virginia*, 388 U.S. 1, 2 (1967), Brief for Appellants.
2. David Goodman Croly, *Miscegenation: The Theory of the Blending of the Races, Applied to the American White Man, and Negro* (Unionville, New York: Royal Fireworks Press, 1995), p. 7.
3. Ibid.
4. Joseph R. Washington, Jr., *Marriage in Black and White* (Lanham, Md.: University Press of America, Inc., 1993), p. 44.
5. A. Leon Higginbotham, Jr., *In the Matter of Color* (New York: Oxford University Press, 1978), p. 44.
6. John David Smith, ed., *Racial Determinism and the Fear of Miscegenation Post-1900: Race and "The Negroe Problem,"* (New York: Garland Publishing, Inc., 1993), p. xii.
7. Ibid.
8. Ibid.
9. Laws of Virginia, (Hening 1823), pp. 86–87.
10. Ibid., p. 87.
11. Ibid.
12. Higginbotham, Jr., p. 10.

13. Virginia Acts of Assembly 1852–1853, chapter 25, p. 40.

14. Virginia Acts of Assembly 1865–1866, chapter 17, section 1, p. 84.

15. Virginia Acts of Assembly 1910, chapter 357, section 49, p. 581.

16. Walter Wadlington, *The Loving Case: Virginia's Anti-Miscegenation Statute in Historical Perspective* (Worcester, Mass.: Virginia Law Review, 1966), vol. 52, p. 1201.

17. Virginia Annotated Law Codes, section 20–58, (1950).

18. Ibid., section 20–59.

19. Deb Price, "Commentary: Civil Wedding Rites," *Gannett News Service*, April 17, 1997, p. 14.

20. *The Slaughter-House Cases*, 83 U.S. (16 Wall.) 36, 71 (1873).

21. A. Leon Higginbotham, Jr., *Shades of Freedom* (New York: Oxford University Press, 1996), pp. 88–89.

## Chapter 2. The Road to the Supreme Court

1. *Loving* v. *Virginia*, 388 U.S. 1, 2 (1967), Record.

2. Ibid.

3. Ed Cray, *Chief Justice: A Biography of Earl Warren* (New York: Simon & Schuster, 1997), p. 449.

4. *Loving* v. *Virginia*, 388 U.S. 1, 6 (1967), Record.

5. Ibid., p. 16.

6. Ibid.

7. Ibid., pp. 16–17.

8. Victoria Valentine, "When Love Was a Crime," *Emerge*, June 30, 1997, p. 60.

9. Peter Irons and Stephanie Guitton, eds.. *May It Please the Court* (New York: The New Press, 1993), p. 278.

10. Charles Lam Markmann, *The Noblest Cry: A History of the American Civil Liberties Union* (New York: St. Martin's Press, 1965), p. 3.

11. *Loving* v. *Virginia,* 388 U.S. 1, 2 (1967).

12. Ibid.

13. 206 Va. 924, 929 (1966).

14. *Loving* v. *Virginia,* 388 U.S. 1, 2 (1967), Brief for Appellee.

15. *Loving* v. *Virginia,* 388 U.S. 1, 3 (1967), Brief for Appellant.

## Chapter 3. A Look at Race-Related Laws

1. *Pace* v. *Alabama,* 106 U.S. 583 (1882).

2. *McLaughlin* v. *Florida,* 379 U.S. 184 (1964).

3. *Naim* v. *Naim,* 350 U.S. 891 (1955).

4. *Pace* v. *Alabama,* 106 U.S. 583 (1882).

5. *Naim* v. *Naim,* 350 U.S. 891 (1955).

6. Ibid.

7. *Brown* v. *Board of Education,* 347 U.S. 483 (1954).

8. Bernard Schwartz, *A History of the Supreme Court* (New York: Oxford University Press, 1993), p. 264.

9. Ed Cray, *Chief Justice: A Biography of Earl Warren* (New York: Oxford University Press, 1993), p. 451.

10. Ibid.

11. Florida Statutes Annotated Section 798.05 (1961).

12. *McLaughlin* v. *Florida* 379 U.S. 184, 192–193 (1964).

13. Paul Johnson, *A History of the American People* (New York: HarperCollins Publishers, 1997), p. 892.

14. Howard Zinn, *A People's History of the United States* (New York: HarperPerennial, 1995), p. 444.

15. Ibid., p. 953.

16. 42 U.S.C Sec. 2000 (1964).

## Chapter 4. The Case for the Lovings

1. Patricia Brennan, "Mixed-Race Couple's Landmark Case on TV," *Minneapolis Star Tribune*, March 30, 1996, p. 6E.

2. *Loving* v. *Virginia*, 388 U.S. 1, 12 (167), Brief for Appellants.

3. Peter Irons and Stephanie Guitton, eds., *May It Please the Court* (New York: The New Press, 1993), pp. 280–281.

4. Walter Wadlington, *The Loving Case: Virginia's Anti-Miscegenation Statute in Historical Perspective* (Worcester, Mass.: Virginia Law Review, 1966), vol. 52, p. 1189.

5. *Journal of the Senate of the Commonwealth of Virginia* (Richmond, Va.: Superintendent of Public Printing, 1924), p. 135.

6. Ernest Sevier Cox, *The South's Part in Mongrelizing the Nation* (Richmond, Va.: White American Society, 1926), p. 98.

7. *Loving* v. *Virginia*, 388 U.S. 1, 23 (1967), Brief for Appellants.

8. Ibid.

9. Ibid.

10. Ibid., p. 24.

11. Ibid., p. 27.

12. Ibid.

13. Ibid., p. 28.

14. *Brown* v. *Board of Education*, 347 U.S. 483 (1954).

15. *Loving* v. *Virginia*, 388 U.S. 1, 31–32 (1967), Brief for Appellants.

16. *Pace* v. *Alabama* 106 U.S. 583 (1883).

17. *Loving* v. *Virginia*, 388 U.S. 1, 32 (1967), Brief for Appellants.

18. *Hamm* v. *Virginia State Board of Elections*, 379 U.S. 19 (1964).

19. *Anderson* v. *Martin*, 375 U.S. 399 (1964).

20. *Watson* v. *City of Memphis*, 373 U.S. 526 (1963).

21. *Hirabayashi* v. *United States*, 320 U.S. 81, 100 (1943).

22. *Loving* v. *Virginia*, 388 U.S. 1, 35 (1967), Brief for Appellants.

23. Ibid.

24. Ibid., p. 36.

25. Ibid.

26. Ibid.

27. Ibid.

28. Ibid., p. 38.

29. *Loving* v. *Virginia*, 388 U.S. 1, 40 (1967), Brief for Appellants.

30. *Loving* v. *Virginia*, 388 U.S. 1 (1967), *Amicus* Brief of John R. Russell, Bishop of Richmond, et. al., p. 6.

31. Ibid., p. 7.

32. Ibid., p. 12.

33. Ibid., p. 13.

34. Ibid., pp. 10–11.

35. Ibid., p. 20.

36. Ibid.

37. Irons and Guitton, p. 281.

## Chapter 5. The Case for Virginia

1. *Loving* v. *Virginia* 388 U.S. 1, 10 (1967), Brief for Appellee.

2. Ibid., p. 15.

3. Ibid., p. 16.

4. Ibid., p. 17.

5. Ibid.

6. Ibid., p. 24.

7. Ibid., p. 27

8. Ibid., p. 7.

9. Ibid., p. 42.

10. Ibid., p. 43.

11. Ibid., p. 47.

12. Ibid., p. 51.

13. *Loving* v. *Virginia*, 388 U.S. 1, 2 (1967), *Amicus* Brief for the State of North Carolina.

14. Ibid., p. 5.

15. Ibid.

16. Ibid., p. 6.

17. Ibid.

## Chapter 6. The Supreme Court's Decision

1. *Loving* v. *Virginia*, 388 U.S. 1, 2–3 (1967).

2. Ibid., p. 7.

3. Ibid., p. 10.

4. Ibid., p. 8.

5. Ibid.

6. Ibid., p. 9.

7. Ibid., p. 10.

8. Ibid.

9. Ibid., p. 11.

10. Ibid.

11. Ibid.

12. Peter Irons and Stephanie Guitton, eds., *May It Please the Court* (New York: The New Press, 1993), p. 286.

13. Ibid.

14. Patricia Brennan, "Mixed-Race Couple's Landmark Case on TV," *Minneapolis Star Tribune*, March 30, 1966, p. 6E.

## Chapter 7. The Impact of the *Loving* Decision

1. Leon Higginbotham, Jr., *Shades of Freedom* (New York: Oxford University Press, 1996), p. 45.

2. Wallace Turner, "Rusk's Daughter, 18, Is Wed to Negro," *The New York Times*, September 22, 1967, p. 1.

3. "Races: A Marriage of Enlightenment," *Time*, September 29, 1967, p. 28.

4. Ibid.

5. Mark Mathabane and Gail Mathabane, *Love in Black and White* (New York: HarperPerennial, 1992), pp. 173–174.

6. Ibid., p. 174.

7. Ibid.

8. Seth Schiessel and Robert L. Turner, "Is Race Obsolete?" *Minneapolis Star Tribune*, October 21, 1996, p. 11A.

9. Helen Bond, "Crossing the Line," *The Dallas Morning News*, January 26, 1999, p. 5C.

10. Ibid.

11. Clayton Majete, "What You May Not Know About Interracial Marriages," vol. 12, *The World & I*, July 1, 1997, p. 300.

12. Lise Funderburg, *Black, White, Other* (New York: William Morrow and Company, Inc., 1994), p. 26.

13. Marlon Manuel, "Black or Not: Interracial Marriage Still an Issue," *The Atlanta Journal and Constitution*, December 20, 1998, p. A8.

14. Ibid.

15. Ibid.

16. Ibid.

# Glossary

**American Civil Liberties Union (ACLU)**—An organization that offers legal assistance to those who believe that their constitutional rights have been violated but cannot afford an attorney.

*amicus curiae*—"Friend of the court," in Latin. A friend of the court is a person or group of people who feel they have information that should be available to the judge during a trial. These people usually have a strong opinion on the case before the court, and wish to have their views known. Friends of the court must ask permission from the judge in order to file a brief.

**annul**—"Undoing" a marriage. Annulment does not end a marriage, but rather declares that, legally, there never was a marriage.

**bail**—Money deposited with the court in order to gain the temporary release of a person who has been arrested.

**caste system**—A social class system in India that was determined by birth.

**Caucasian**—A "white" person.

**civil rights**—Those rights guaranteed to the individual by amendments to the United States Constitution.

**due process**—Going through the usual legal processes provided by law. Due process requires that the government follow all the rules meant to protect an individual's rights. In a criminal case, the requirements of due process would include the right to a trial by jury.

**equal protection**—A constitutional guarantee that no person or group of people will be treated differently under the law from any other person or group of people.

**evasion statute**—A law that makes it a separate crime to leave a particular state to engage in conduct that would be illegal in that state and then returning to that state.

**felony**—The most serious level of crime. Of the many freedoms enjoyed by Americans, felons lose their right and freedom to vote.

**Fourteenth Amendment**—Amendment to the United States Constitution that guarantees all Americans equal protection under the law, regardless of race.

**indentured servant**—A person bound by a contract to work for another. The servant was usually only one step above a slave, in that there was a fixed period of time that the contract lasted. Such arrangements were sometimes made to pay off a debt that the servant owed to the master.

**interracial**—Between the races. An interracial marriage would involve a marriage between people of different races—for instance, one white and one black partner.

**invidious discrimination**—Giving offense by discriminating unfairly.

**Jim Crow**—Discrimination against, or segregation of, African Americans through a series of laws.

**miscegenation**—marriage or cohabitation between a white person and a member of another race.

**Nazi party**—The political party that ruled Germany under Adolf Hitler during World War II.

**Roman Catholic Church**—One of the Christian churches, headed by the Pope.

# Further Reading

Cray, Ed. *Chief Justice: A Biography of Earl Warren*. New York: Simon & Schuster, 1997.

Emert, Phyllis R. *Top Lawyers and Their Famous Cases*. Minneapolis, Minn.: Oliver Press, Inc., 1996.

Herda, D.J. *Earl Warren: Chief Justice for Social Change*. Springfield, N.J.: Enslow Publishers, Inc., 1995.

Higginbotham, Jr., A. Leon. *Shades of Freedom*. New York: Oxford University Press, 1996.

Kelly, Zachary A. *Trials and Sentences*. Vero Beach, Fla.: Rourke Publications, Inc., 1998.

Kull, Andrew. *The Color-Blind Constitution*. Cambridge, Mass.: Harvard University Press, 1994.

McLynn, Frank. *Famous Trials: Cases That Made History*. New York: The Reader's Digest Association, Inc., 1995.

## Internet Addresses

American Law Sources On-Line
<http://www.lawsource.com>

American Civil Liberties Union
<http://www.aclu.org/>

Association of Multi-Ethnic Americans
<http://www.ameasite.org/index.html>

University of California at Berkeley Library Resources on Interracial Marriage and People of Mixed Race
<http://lib.berkeley.edu/TeachingLib/Guides/MixedRace.html>

# Index